THE PATHWAY
TO
WISDOM

Heb. 3:17-19

Ernie Perkins

Ernie Perkins, Th.D., D.Min.

In Memory of my dad,
Lilborn E. Perkins, Sr.,
the first of many
sages who enriched my
life.

Published by
Encounter Publishing Company
Oklahoma City, Oklahoma
Copyright 1997

Ernie Perkins
5209 S. E. 46th Street
Oklahoma City, Oklahoma 73135
ernieperkins@Juno.com

CONTENTS

THE PATHWAY TO WISDOM
Ernie Perkins

FOREWORD

We can interpret mankind's history from one of two positions. These two positions are the world's view and the Biblical view.

The world's view sees man as a mountain climber, climbing out of the swamps and mushes of prehistoric animal characteristics on his way to utopia at the top of Mt. Self-Achievement. Man is ever evolving upward toward perfection.

The Biblical view sees man as a rider in a roller-coaster car. He was placed on the top of perfection by a God of grace. There, perfect in every way, physical, mental, as well as spiritual, man, forgetting who he was and in an effort to become like God, cut himself off from the chain of God's fellowship that had placed him on that first high hill. When he cut that chain, man found himself on a wild ride, alternating between ups and downs until the present hour.

There were times when spiritual revivals and awakenings took man upward for a short distance, but then he would shoot down a hill of rebellion and sin. There have been times when it appeared that the next curve would be unmanageable and mankind would go plunging over the rail to death and destruction. Yet, so far, some- how, the car has remained on the track and is still moving. However, even the casual observer will detect that the upward hills are not as pronounced as they have been in past history, and while the track is becoming smoother with fewer and less pronounced inclines, it is definitely declining at a fast-falling downward pace. Many of us believe the getting-off place is just ahead.

If ever there has been a time when we need wise men and women in every avenue of our society, it is today.

Plato, without the benefit of the divine revelation of God's word, saw wisdom as having three aspects. First, there was the wisdom that was a gift given from outside of mankind to special men. Second, there was the practical wisdom that the statesmen and leaders of the community needed. And, third, there was the scientific wisdom of the inventors and changers.

Plato had great insight.

During the past few years, there has been a remarkable renewed interest in the study of wisdom. For years, it was considered a part of the metaphysical, and as such, it was placed in the same category as "sin" and "eternal truth." For most secular writers, man's upward climb had moved him out of such misty and antique notions, into the cloud-free upper atmosphere of truth that did not need such superstitious answers to man's problems and needs.

Even in the religious world, many have tried to marry their theology with a worldly philosophy and, as a result, have lost their cutting edge.

"Philosophy" can be defined as a "world view," or a statement as to how one views the world and his or her part in that world.

"Theology" is basically a "God's view," or a statement as to how one views God and his or her relationship to God.

While many argue that one's philosophy can be separated from one's theology, I personally do not see how it can. A person's view of God will determine his or her view of the world. And most people have both a theology and a philosophy, expressed verbally or not.

Many, not understanding the difference between principle and philosophy, confuse the two. Ask the average person what his or her personal philosophy is and you will get such answers as: "Do unto others, as you would have them do unto you," or "My philosophy is the ten commandments."

These are great principles by which to live, but philosophy is a larger umbrella than either of these statements.

Basically, philosophy can be divided into three large general groups. Most people build their personal mission statements, life's goals, or whatever they call the personal principles by which they govern their lives onto the framework of one of these basic philosophies.

These three philosophies are the Essentialist Philosophy, the Pragmatic Philosophy, and the Existentialist Philosophy. The following story illustrates them:

The presidents of three institutions of higher learning got into an argument concerning which of the three schools produced the smartest graduate. One school was a theological seminary, the second was a school of medicine, and the third was a law school.

They decided to take a recent doctoral graduate from each of their schools and give them all the same test to see which was the smartest.

So, they asked the young doctor of ministry graduate from the seminary, "Tell us, how much is two plus two?"

Without a moment's hesitation, the young theologue answered, "Four."

Then, they asked the young medical doctor, "Tell us, how much is two plus two?"

The young doctor thought for a long while, looked carefully at the first two and then at the second two, before moving on to study intently the plus sign, and then he turned and said, "I'm not sure until I run some tests."

They asked the young lawyer the same question, "How much," they asked, "is two plus two?"

The young lawyer answered, "How much do you want it

to be?"

The three presidents were not able to agree which student was the smartest because each president claimed that his student had given the right answer.

And, depending upon their different philosophies, each student's answer would have been considered correct.

"How much is two plus two?" To the Essentialist Philosopher, the answer will always be "four." To the Essentialist, Truth is spelled with the capital letter. The Essentialist believes there are essential Truths given to the human race by God and that these essential Truths do not change. They may be rejected, but even if rejected, they do not change. They are still Truths. The conservative Christian is an Essentialist in his or her philosophy.

"How much is two plus two?" To the Pragmatic Philosopher, the answer will depend upon what the community thinks. To the Pragmatic, there are no definite truths. Truths change as do people. Things that were considered wrong by a previous generation, if accepted by the current generation, are no longer wrong. Homosexuality, for example, is an accepted lifestyle by a certain city; therefore, it is not wrong if the people have accepted it. To the Pragmatic, "If it works, it's good." In the moral sense, the statement can be translated, "If it feels good and doesn't hurt anyone, then it is good." The Pragmatic places emphases on the person, personal experiences, and inductive reasoning.

"How much is two plus two?" To the Existentialist, two plus two is whatever the individual believes it to be. There are no absolutes and no eternal truths. Truth is whatever the Existentialist has discovered it to be in his or her situation. Therefore, everything is situational. Truth is impossible to know outside a context, and the context is the determiner of truth.

The conservative Christian lives in a large spiritual

housing development called "Christianity." However, he is discovering that many living in that development have brought in the Pragmatic and Existential Philosophies, and there is no unity with his neighbors.

Some, while trying to live under the name of Christianity, still accept "truth" as being whatever works. The world has changed and if some new "truth" has been discovered, it is accepted as more true than that · which is old. Recent generations have "proven" the theory of evolution, if not by facts, certainly by desire, and have moved beyond the superstitions of earlier generations. The Pragmatic Christian, in his attempt to justify his faith with the current understanding of scientific truth, has cut himself off from the Eternal Truths of God's Word.

In an effort, for example, to accept the new and therefore "true" science of evolution while simultaneously holding on to their Truth of God, many Christians proclaim themselves "Theistic Evolutionists." So what if science has now "proven" that man is a product of evolution, God is the cause and the director of that evolution. Thus, the Truth of God's Word becomes fable, teaching the greater truth that God is the cause. Truth becomes whatever the newest fad proclaims it to be, and the Pragmatic Christian will mold his beliefs around it.

Perhaps more dangerous than the acceptance of pragmatic philosophy by the Christian community, has been an acceptance of the Existentialist Philosophy. Existentialism has invaded the ranks of Christianity far more than most realize. Within my own denomination, Southern Baptists, many would consider themselves Bible believing conservatives theologically, but are Existentialists in philosophy. These Existentialists march under the banner, "The Priesthood of the Believer," which is a cherished Southern Baptist doctrine. Nevertheless, as in any doctrine, it can be polluted, and it has been by many. When a church's decision to ordain

9

homosexuals is defended in the name of "priesthood of the believer," the doctrine is being polluted. Those who make the "priesthood of the believer" doctrine to be another way to march under the Existentialist Philosophy have forgotten one very important fact of Old Testament History. There was no other office in the Old Testament that had more restrictions placed upon it than did the priesthood. It rested under the continual judgment of God and man. The doctrine of the priesthood of the believer is not a license to do whatever one would like to do, or believe whatever one would like to believe. It is a doctrine that says man needs no other mediator than Christ. In the Old Testament book of Judges, there is a recurring statement that described the chaos of that area of Jewish history. "In those days Israel had no king and *every man did that which was right in his own eyes.*" The idea of doing whatever one would like to do without being held accountable by the community of believers is as destructive now as it was in the days of the Judges.

If ever human society has needed men and women of wisdom who can give wise leadership, it is today. Yet, in an area when knowledge has never been more revered, true wisdom seems to be a scarce commodity. At a time when more people hold more degrees from more institutions than at any other point in human history, we join with those in the fable who searched through their city for a wise man . . . and found none.

Where is wisdom, and where are the wise?

God Word says, *"If any of you lack wisdom, let him ask of God, that giveth to all men liberally, and upbraideth not; and it shall be given him,"* James 1:5.

The implication of this verse is that wisdom should be a normal part of Christian maturity. The promise is to anyone who *lacks* wisdom, not to anyone who *desires* or *wants* wisdom. It implies that all should have wisdom, that it is a natural, perhaps supernatural, part of the Christian process toward maturity. Yet, wisdom is scarce in our society, even among God's people. But why is that? Is the pathway to wisdom so hidden that it cannot be found?

When I was a boy, I lived in the Mississippi River Valley of North Arkansas, far from any city or town.

It was easy to see the stars in those earlier days of my life. However, I don't see the stars much anymore. It isn't that I am not out at night. I'm there, and they are there, but their brightness is hidden by the glare of man-made street lights.

By the same way, heavenly things like wisdom can be hidden by the glares of man-made philosophies and ideas. If we are to discover wisdom, we will have to begin with the eternal truths of God's word.

How can we get past the clutter of our worldly, carnal life- styles and find the wisdom that God has said that we are to have? What are the components of wisdom, and what is the pathway that will take us to it?

The Bible's Book of Wisdom, Proverbs, has more to say about wisdom than does any other book. It would be appropriate for us to look for our answers there.

In Proverbs, chapter two, two very important words should be examined in connection with wisdom.

My son, if thou wilt receive my words, and hide my commandments with thee; So that thou incline thine ear unto wisdom, and apply thine heart to understand; Yea, if thou criest after knowledge, and liftest up thy voice for understanding; If thou seekest her as silver, and searchest for her as for hid treasures; Then shalt thou understand the fear of the Lord, and find the knowledge of God. For the Lord giveth wisdom: out of his mouth cometh knowledge and understanding.

The two words connected with the word *wisdom* in these verses are *knowledge* and *understanding*. On our pathway to wisdom, these words will play a big part in helping us achieve the wisdom that God's word says we should have.

Wisdom is more than intelligence, but it does include intelligence. Intelligence is the ability to learn, and knowledge in the measurable substance of intelligence. Until there is knowledge, there is no indication or proof of intelligence. It is only when one can determine that knowledge has taken place that there can be proof of intelligence.

Proud parents rejoice to see their little baby learning at an apparent genius level during those first few years of life. "If only we could continue to learn at that amazing level for the rest of our lives," we say. However, it should be remembered that during those first years, the child's little mind is empty and is crying out for knowledge. Just as things rush to a vacuum, so does knowledge rush to the mind of a child. And, while we may not be able to continue learning at the rate that we did when we first began the learning process, there is no reason why we should not desire to keep learning.

However, we say, "It isn't my fault that I can't learn."

Or, "I wasn't given an opportunity to learn."

Or, "I can't help it if I'm stupid."

Many are prone to give knowledge a life of its own, as if it comes and goes, smiles and frowns, awakes or sleeps purely on its own terms to those few who are blessed enough to receive it. If they cannot control knowledge, who can then? So, they blame it on circumstances.

Knowledge is not an irresistible, uncontrollable, outside force over which we have no control.

It is a mystery, but it is understandable, if not in whole, at least in part.

Knowledge can be controlled, attained, and reinforced. But, it can also be prevented and stopped.

While most philosophies would agree that knowledge is manageable, as a conservative Essentialist Christian, I acknowledge the absolute Truths as found within the Word of God. My Essentialist belief that the human mind learns, even if it is not acted upon at the moment, gives me tremendous personal influence over my own reservoir of knowledge. I do have the power to add to that reservoir of knowledge, and if I remain in relatively good health, I can continue adding to it for the rest of my life.

CHAPTER ONE

KNOWLEDGE:
The Acquiring of Information

The human mind is a reservoir, a cistern, it is not a well. Of itself, it cannot generate knowledge without resources with which to work.

A brief explanation of the difference between a cistern and a well will better explain my meaning. A well is a hole dug into the ground to reach a source of water. It can produce water from within. Indeed, it is its own source of water.

A cistern, on the other hand, is a hole dug into the ground to become a storage tank. It has no source of water of its own, but only becomes a reservoir for water placed within it. If the human mind is a reservoir like a cistern, then it must receive its "water," knowledge, from outside sources.

The outside sources, or "pools," from which knowledge comes are reason, intuition, common sense, experience, experts, and revelation. The pipes, or "conduits," through which knowledge moves from the pools to the reservoir of the mind are the five senses of hearing, seeing, tasting, touching, and smelling, plus the sixth sense of spirit. Each healthy child is born with a mind to be filled, and each healthy child begins life with the five physical senses through which it receives knowledge. To the extent that either of these senses is impaired, it is to that extent that the child must overcome a handicap to the filling (learning) process. The child with no sight will have to use the other conduits to make up for that which he or she would have learned through sight. Those children who suffer both sight and hearing loss (Helen Keller being a well-known illustration), have extreme difficulties to overcome. Yet, as Miss Keller proved, these difficulties can be overcome, and the reservoir can be filled. She did learn, because Miss Anne Sullivan, her teacher, penetrated the darkness of blindness and deafness to reach her through the sense of touch, and the story of Helen Keller's associating water with the marking that her teacher was placing on her hand is legendary. If, however, Miss Keller had lost her other senses of touch, smell, and taste, there would have been absolutely no way that she could have ever learned anything. Her mind, which proved to be brilliant, would have been closed to all avenues through which knowledge could enter, and her brilliance would have been lost.

As one increases in age, the conduits can lose some of their sharpness. It short, they become clogged. People can and should add to their reservoir throughout their lives. Yet, many older people can be tempted to yield to the temptation to live their latter years drawing from their reservoir instead of adding to it. Because the older person's conduits can become clogged, it becomes easy to accept perceived limitations. The clogging of the conduits can be either physical or psychological. But either can effectively cause older adults to stop learning before he or she stops living. That is a tragedy of some people's growing older.

A few years ago, Carol Barnett had one of the most popular shows on television. Miss Barnett's strength lay with her abilities to portray the funny side of people, groups, and situations. A partial list of these groups included married couples, mothers-in-law and mothers, children, dating couples, and older people. While it must be remembered that comedy works best through exaggeration, her portrayal of the elderly (along with that of her co-star Tim Conway) pictured them as spiteful, ill-tempered, slow moving, living in the past, absent minded, hard of hearing, and senile. Unfortunately, although the names of television shows have changed, the projected image of elderly people generally has not.

Carol Barnett's and Tim Conway's routines were only a small part of a general impression that has not changed. Many older adults have accepted this general impression, and their acceptance has produced psychological barriers to learning that become greater than the physical barriers. In fact, if most older adults can get victory over the psychological barriers to learning, they will find a way to overcome the physical barriers. These psychological barriers are those false assumptions, accusations, or myths that "everyone knows;" and unfortunately most older adults seem ready to accept these as true. The following conclusions were based upon the premise that the adult was in relatively good health.

The first of these myths is the "You can't teach an old dog new tricks" myth. Whoever first reached this conclusion did not know anything about dogs. And those who would apply this to older adults and their ability to learn, do not know anything about adult education. The research studies do not give credence to this proverb. People can learn throughout their life span. However, many older people refuse to accept the facts, and instead have accepted the myth that learning new things is beyond their abilities. Researchers in education today realize that there is very little decline in the ability to learn as one grows older. The tests, it has been realized, were unintentionally developed to favor the younger person. As a result, the earlier conclusions that learning skills lessened as age increased were wrong. It is now known that older people can do very well on tests if their age characteristics are taken into consideration.

For example, most tests that measure intelligence and learning skills are timed tests. The participant is given more questions that anyone could possibly answer, and they are given a certain period of time to answer as many as possible. The younger person will move quickly through the test, answering each question rather quickly and moving to the next. There are two reasons for their speed. One, their reservoir of experience and knowledge is not nearly as full as is the older adult. Therefore, they quickly draw an answer from their limited reservoir and move to the next question. Older adults, however, become naturally more cautious as they age, and do not quickly reach conclusions. In addition, they have a much larger reservoir of experiences and knowledge from which to draw an answer; thus, they moved through the test much slower than the young adults. Their increased caution and larger reservoir express themselves in fewer answers over the period of the test. With fewer answers over a period of time, the interpretation of slower learning skills and intelligence is falsely assumed.

Another myth would have us believe that people become grouchy and cantankerous as they become old. This may, or may not, be true. Emotionally, the older adult is only an extension of what he or she was when younger. Aging is not something that suddenly begins at a particular birthday. All of the experiences that we have had and all the personal characteristics that are ours lead us to the door of who we will be in our old age. In the movies, <u>Grumpy Old Men</u> and <u>Grumpier Old Men</u>, the characters played by Jack Lemmon and Walter Matthau were only expressions of their younger selves. Age of itself does not make a person mean; it only gives the mean person an opportunity to perfect through experience and practice his or her mean nature. In the same way, age of itself does not make a saint. The older good person is a person who is extending through a lifetime of being that which the person is. Unless there is a supernatural spiritual intervention or a change in health, the human personality changes very little. The younger person with a zest for life will be an older person with a zeal for living. The youthful complainer will become an old gripe. Old age just gives a person the opportunity to practice what that person has always been, to become perfect at it. Stated simply, then as one is, one generally remains, only more so. This is a reason, for the young adult to find someone of whom he or she can say, "I want to be like that when I am that age." And then to realize as my wife told me after hearing a similar statement from me, "Ernie, in order to be like that then, you have to start now."

Another myth relating to older people is the charge that they live too much in the past. However, people's time orientation can be influenced by many factors such as their environment, their heritage, their personality, as well as their age. Some people, no matter their age, live in the past. Others live only for the moment. Yet others have a future time orientation. The truth is older adults do not live in the past any more than do younger adults. There is very little difference between the thirty-year-old granddaughter and the seventy-six-year-old grandmother at this point. If one were to listen, unobservably, to the conversation of a group of thirty-year-old women and count the number of past tense verbs used in the group's conversation, and compare it with a similar group of older ladies' use of past tense verbs, the percentage of difference would be minute. The difference, of course, would be that the thirty-year-old ladies would be talking about something that happened yesterday, or last week, whereas the grandmothers may be talking about something that happened twenty or thirty years ago. But past tense verbs are expressions of the past, regardless of how long ago the past was. Older people do not talk about the past any more than do any other generation, though the past that they do talk about is naturally of a longer duration.

Older people do become more practical concerning things as they age. The older man will not see any point in throwing away a perfectly good tie that he has enjoyed simply because it is last year's model. Things stay "new" longer for the older person than they do for his or her younger counterpart. When a year represents only one- seventy-fifth of one's life, it is a shorter period than when it represents one-twentieth of one's life. Thus, it is harder for the older person to realize how quickly clothing styles change, and they can become guilty of wearing clothes that the younger generation would consider outdated.

One myth that is all too often accepted by most is the statement, "I must be getting old. I can't remember anything anymore." The idea is that growing older automatically means becoming more forgetful. But this is not necessarily so. The older person adds to this concept by fussing that "I'm sorry that I can't remember your name. I'm getting so forgetful." But is the older people's inability to remember someone's name a matter of age and forgetfulness? I think not.

If my twenty-five-year-old son and I were to attend the same party tonight, meet the same number of people, and then compare notes tomorrow, he may be able to remember the names of more of our new acquaintances than I. However, it is only logical that he should. There are two reasons for this.

One, most of us, as we get older, develop the ability to let things pass that we feel will not be useful to us in the future. Therefore, many of us do not pay attention when introduced to those whom we feel may be a one-time meeting. We don't remember the name because we never "membered" it in the first place. How can we "re" what we have never done? Actually, we probably need not wait until tomorrow to confess that we don't know it; we probably couldn't repeat it after two minutes. It isn't a matter of remembering. It is simply a matter of not paying attention.

The second reason is just as simple, yet, just as real. When I consciously try to remember a name, it joins the thousands of other names that I have already placed in my memory bank. Therefore, when my son and I are drawing from our memory, he is drawing from far fewer names than I. It is always easier to find one item from among one thousand than it is to find that same item hidden among tens of thousands.

These two reasons for forgetting have their antidotes. First, if the older person has trouble remembering simple actions such as whether or not he or she has turned off the coffee maker or remembering where the keys were laid, the person needs to realize that again the problem isn't forgetfulness nearly as much as it is not paying attention. The action was not remembered because it was a habit action. Most of these things are thoughtlessly done without any efforts made to place the actions into the memory mode. If one wants to remember that the coffee maker is turned off, then one should consciously make the effort. One way to do this is by "Declarative Memory." Declarative memory is to declare aloud as one turns off the coffer maker, "The coffee maker is off." The action of declaring the action moves it from the habit mode to the memory mode. My wife and I have trouble "remembering" if we let down our garage door or not. Now, Wanda and I declare as the garage door is coming down, "The garage door is going down. The garage door is now completely down." By a spoken declaration, we no longer have to ask two miles down the road, "Did we close the garage door?"

Drawing things from a memory enlarged by time and experience is not always easy, but it is not to be a cause of concern. The older adult needs to understand this and accept it. He or she should realize that there are many things more important to remember than a dentist appointment that is still two weeks away. There are children and grandchildren's many friends, birthdays, anniversaries, addresses, and phone numbers that now are a part of their lives that were not when they were younger. Memory is like a muscle. Don't use it and you can lose it no matter the age. But if it is activated and worked, stretched and expanded, used and exercised, it can stay at its full strength and even improve.

"Older people don't like change," claims a leading church growth expert. He is just another of the many who give credence to the myth; however, he is wrong.

No other generation has experienced more change than has the generation now designated as the "old" generation. To lay a charge that they don't like change is to deny everything that has happened to them for decades.

Yet, if the charge isn't true, how does one explain its being made so often?

It is not change that the older folks are afraid of. It is the fear of the loss of control. Older people are continuously fighting to maintain control of their lives and things.

A daughter, now living in Houston, fusses because her widowed mother will not sell her home in Oklahoma City and move to Houston. In the ongoing joking spirit between Texans and Okies, the mother gives her explanation, "Honey, I got saved so that I won't have to go to Hell." But it doesn't satisfy the daughter. Mom's unyielding defiance is seen as one more example of an older person who just won't change, instead of correctly being seen as one is trying to maintain control of her life. One of the greatest fears of growing older is the fear of growing physically weaker and increasingly dependent. Senior adults want to postpone their loss of control as long as possible. In their effort to remain in control, they are falsely accused of being against change. The charge is not true.

"The old boy just can't cut the mustard anymore." "Bless his heart. He has lost it." These and other statements like them infer that age makes one less than what that one has been in the past. Of course, one will lose physical strength as one gets older, but the simple fact is the more one uses what one has the longer than one will keep it. The key to continual ability to do, is continually to do. The more one maintains an active physical, mental, emotional, and social life, the longer that one will be able to enjoy life and make contributions to it.

If one can get victory over these psychological barriers to life- long learning, one can usually find a way to get around the physical barriers.

Of course, as a person gets older, that person's physical strengths and physical senses of hearing, seeing, and the other three will become weaker. This weakness can be referred to as the physical cause for the clogging of the conduits by which information moves from its source to the reservoir of the mind in older adults. If the older person does not let foolish pride stand in the way of finding ways by which the failing of the senses can be overcome, that older person can continue to learn.

For example, when I first started wearing glasses, I was a young teen-aged kid whose glasses placed me in a minority, but now most people my age, fifty-eight, need glasses. If I permit my pride to keep me from wearing glasses, I will be limiting myself to a major avenue of learning.

We also begin to lose our sense of taste. This needs to be a matter of awareness by the older person, but not necessarily a matter of concern. Because the sweet buds are the last to go, many older people find that they are enjoying their desserts more, and as a result, start eating more sweets than is good for them. If one destroys his or her health by eating too many sweets, then obviously that one will be curtailing his or her ability to learn.

Most older people will limit themselves more at the point of hearing loss than any other sense lost. Hearing loss is a major problem for the older person that not only affects him or her physically, but also affects their relationship with others.

There has traditionally been a lack of sensitivity to the problem of the loss of hearing, which Beethoven identified as his "noblest faculty." Many do not understand the dimensions of hearing loss. Many people of any age group may suffer from hearing loss. They live under continuous pressure to translate what they hear so they can answer questions correctly and carry their part of conversations without appearing foolish. However, people have a greater degree of hearing loss as they get older. One expert believes that two out of every three people older than 65 suffer some degree of deafness. In one out of every six cases, the impairment is significant enough to interfere with everyday communication. However, a loss of hearing does not represent a loss of intelligence in any age group, including the older age group.

The last sense that begins to weaken is the sense of smell. When I discovered this, I made a pack with my two sons that one of us will make sure that their mother, my Wanda, will receive a bottle of perfume every Christmas. That way when I can no longer see her, or hear her, I can sniff her out.

While Wisdom may be found in people of all ages, the fact remains that a large disproportional percentage of those considered "wise" by their community are older adults. Age alone does not bring wisdom, but age does give the person an opportunity to perfect what he or she has always been. Therefore, the young adult considered "wise" will become more wise as he or she gets older if . . . and this "if" is an extremely big word . . . if that person overcomes the psychological and physical barriers, and continues to add to his or her reservoir of knowledge. However, it can become a strong temptation to start living from that which is known and to stop learning. Learning should be a life-long endeavor, and for the "wise" person, it is.

CHAPTER TWO

UNDERSTANDING:
The Applying of Information

Although Wisdom contains knowledge, it is more than knowledge. Chapter Five will discuss what happens when one gains knowledge without gaining understanding. However, at this juncture, I want to discuss the second ingredient of wisdom as I believe it is emphasized by God's Word. This second ingredient is Understanding, and it is the harder of the two ingredients to explain.

As revelation (the Word of God) separates and confirms "Truth" from all the information received into the mind from the other five sources (reason, intuition, common sense, experts, and experience), so the Spirit of God teaches the understanding of that which is "Truth."

In knowledge we receive a lot of information that is not "truth" and we must filter all information by the Word of God to determine that which is true from that which is not. So, in Understanding, we comprehend a lot of information that is not "truth," and we need a teacher to help us understand Truth from those things that are not. For example, just as I can know the theory of evolution, I can also move to an understanding of that theory. I can even apply some of its teachings in understanding the evolution of an idea or action, yet I must reject it as the cause for mankind's existence.

All of us are like children in that we can learn far more than we can understand. For the first several years of our lives, we are acquiring much more knowledge than we are applying. This remains true all the way to our adult years. We spend all of our childhood preparing ourselves for the future. The first grader is preparing for the second grade. The second grader is preparing for the third grade, and on it goes throughout the school years. Toward the end of our childhood, we start preparing ourselves for our careers and future jobs. Most of this preparation is the acquiring of information.

There is, however, the necessity to move information from the mind to the heart . . . from the reservoir into the real world of experience. The process of understanding and applying information can be developed and activated by the Spirit of God through several different methods.

One method is the supernatural work of the Holy Spirit. This work cannot be explained. It happens during moments when the Spirit of God shines on the Word of God to reveal a Work of God that we have never understood before. One example of many such moments is when I came to a new understanding of I Timothy 2:1-3 recently. I read the Bible through each year and have done so for the past thirty years. Therefore, I know that I had read these verses many times. In fact, I have even preached sermons from this text. Nevertheless, recently while I was meditating upon these verses, I discovered something I had never seen before. I had always used this text as the basis for good Christian citizenship, but I suddenly understood that it went further than just Christian citizenship. The kings and all that were in authority in Paul's day were making life hard for the Christians. These governmental officials were their persecutors and abusers. The principle, therefore, goes further than just praying for our governmental leaders. It is a challenge for us to pray for all those who treat us in a persecuting and abusing manner. This can include fellow workers at the factory, or the obnoxious neighbor down the street, or the rude driver in the car in the outside lane. I had known the text, but by the Spirit of God, I had come to understand something about it I had never realized. I had learned to apply it in a greater context than I previously had. My knowledge had gained understanding.

We also gain understanding through our experiences and circumstances. However, despite the popularity of the statement, "Experience is the best teacher," it is not. Of itself an experience cannot be. The Christian Essentualist would agree with Aquinas that everything we observe in the world can be argued back to a prime mover, a first cause, or a great designer. The Christian knows that this first cause is God. Therefore, God can, and does, use experiences to teach us, but experiences are but God's curriculum. While not all experiences could be called "good" of themselves, the Christian finds comfort in knowing that "All things work together for good to them that love God." Therefore, even the worst of circumstances can move one from the knowledge that grace is sufficient to experiencing the reality and understanding that grace is indeed sufficient. Many are those who have gained understanding of the grace of God through heartbreaks. Through experience, their knowledge had become understanding.

Another great avenue by which the Spirit of God can move things from my reservoir of knowledge into my area of understanding is His use of godly people. It probably was an indication of my own lack of maturity more than an adequate evaluation of the contents of the sermons I heard, but it does seem to me that there are many more preachers today who share "principles" found within the Word of God than there were when I was a youth. Some of my greatest insights into the understanding of Biblical truths have come by listening to the preaching of God's prophets. If one wants to add to his or her understanding level, that one would do well to make it a habit to listen to men who are well known for their biblical insight. With television, radio, tapes, and the printed word, there is no exercise for one not to take advantage of this tremendous opportunity for growth in understanding.

But, the prophet does not have to be some well known preacher. It can be anyone who has grown in their relationship with their Lord. One of my most understandably profound truths came one Sunday while I was sitting in an adult Sunday School class that a layman was teaching. And the statement didn't even come from the prepared teacher, but from another class member. To the speaker, it was just a passing comment on some of the lesson's material, but the Spirit of God used his statement to give me an insight into faith that I had never realized. God used that layman to move knowledge into understanding.

Understanding can come slowly, or it can be as a lightening flash.

One of my best friends shared with me a new understanding he had received in his study of Proverbs 13:10, *"Only by pride cometh contention."* I first received his information on this verse as knowledge, though he was trying to share with me the understanding. One would think that the verse is simple enough that understanding would come with the knowledge, yet for some reason, my physical mind could not accept the simplicity of the statement *"Only* by pride cometh contention." Yes, pride is *probably one* of the reasons by which contentions come, I reasoned, but surely not the *only* reason. Yet, God's spirit would not let me get the verse from my mind. My friend's words kept coming back until one day the full impact of that simple statement hit me full force. And knowledge had become understanding.

CHAPTER THREE

THE LIFE-LEARNING MATRIX: Placing "Knowledge" and "Understanding" in Perspective

I guess I collect college degrees as a hobby. I don't play golf, and if a person doesn't play golf, it is amazing how much time he can have for other things. I have two bachelors, two masters, two earned doctorates, and I am currently working on my third doctorate in the school of Occupational and Adult Education at Oklahoma State University. It has been during this third doctoral study that I have become fascinated with wisdom. From my reading in the subject area, I became convinced that the secular writers were missing the two major components of wisdom. Their works were hitting all around them, but none (at least that I had found) were correctly identifying them. It needs to be said, however, that the Bible tells us of two wisdoms. Those who are writing from the secular position are trying to find secular answers to a spiritual event. Therefore, their task is stupendous.

Note the difference between secular wisdom and spiritual wisdom as they are defined in James 3:13-18.

Who is a wise man and endued with knowledge among you? Let him shew out of a good conversation his works with meekness of wisdom.

But if ye have bitter envying and strife in your hearts, glory not, and lie not against the truth.

This wisdom descendeth not from above, but is earthly, sensual, devilish.

For where envying and strife is, there is confusion and every evil work.

But the wisdom that is from above is first pure, then peaceable, gentle, and easy to be intreated, full of mercy and good fruits, without partiality, and without hypocrisy. And the fruit of righteousness is sown in peace to them that make peace.

Because real wisdom, at least the type that I was interested in, was the spiritual wisdom, I found that by approaching wisdom theologically as well as educationally, I had found what the others were searching for.

Some had said that wisdom includes personality characteristics, and they were right. However, approaching their studies from the secular, they failed to understand where and how the personality concepts are developed in the truly wise person.

Some had almost made wisdom to be an extremely smart person. Gain knowledge, they implied, and you will automatically gain wisdom. While they were right in their implication that wisdom contains knowledge, they were wrong if they felt that wisdom was but knowledge amplified.

Others had discovered a very pragmatic, practical aspect to wisdom, and these, too, were right. However, the biblical use of the word "understanding" is the better word to describe that which they were trying to define.

As the wisdom concept kept developing in my mind and heart, I realized I needed a visual tool with which to work. From that realization, I developed the Life-Learning Matrix (Figure 1).

The Life-Learning Matrix started out being a large "L" with a Zero at the point where the horizontal bar and the vertical bar connected. There were a series of numbers running up and across the two bars. I tried using the many different ideas for identifying these two ingredients to wisdom,

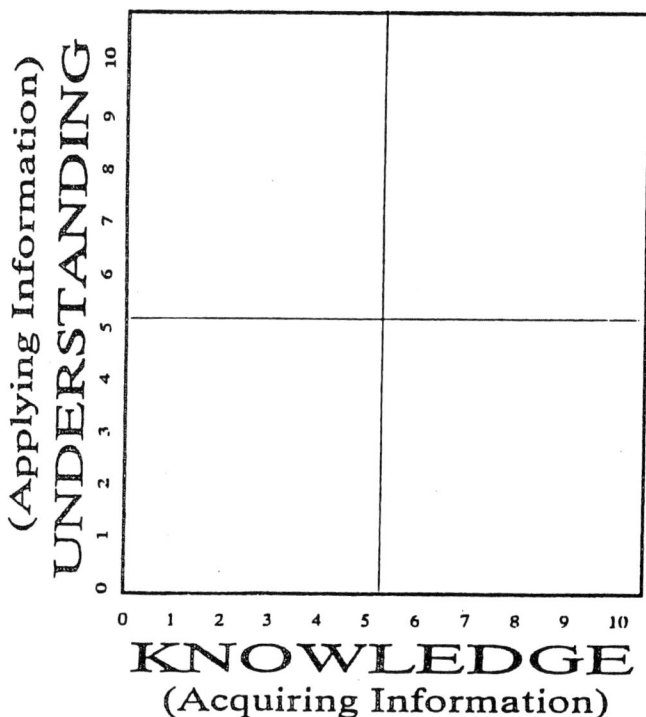

FIGURE 1

but none that I found satisfied me until I felt the freedom to introduce my secular educational endeavors to what I believed was the biblical concept of wisdom. And thus, I named the horizontal bar "Knowledge," and the vertical bar "Understanding."

"Knowledge" and "Understanding"--how did these two relate? And what were the characteristics in the person who was weak in both, or who was strong in one while being weak in the other? Was such a thing possible? Last of all, what were the characteristics of the person who was strong both in knowledge and in wisdom?

The following chapters will attempt to answer these questions.

CHAPTER FOUR

QUADRANT ONE:
The Baby Christian Stage

Just as everyone starts their intellectual life in quadrant one, so does every Christian start his or her Christian life in quadrant one. Unfortunately, many will never leave this quadrant. It takes work and opportunities to advance across the knowledge line and upward on the understanding line. There are many who never find either the challenge or opportunity. Many others are physically or mentally impaired and will never advance very far in either area.

It takes a certain amount of knowledge for one to become a Christian. Paul asks, "How can they call upon Him in whom they have not believed? And how can they believe on Him in whom they have not heard? And how can they hear, unless there is a preacher?" In these series of questions, Paul implies that there is the need to hear. That there is a need to know about God in order to believe in God. While the amount of knowledge needed may be small (I myself could not have quoted a verse of scripture if my soul had depended upon it at the time of my own salvation), some knowledge is necessary. And just as surely as some knowledge is necessary, it is also necessary that there be some understanding. It is not enough just to know that "God so loved the world that He gave . . ." there must be an understanding that "God so loved *me* that He gave . . ." Until the understanding comes to me, I will not see my need for a personal relationship with Christ. Again, the amount of understanding may be minute, but a certain degree of understanding is necessary.

Man has tremendous control over his own knowledge and

some control over his understanding in the area of secular information. However, while it may be possible for man to know about God, it is impossible for man to know God personally and to come to any understanding of spiritual truths except by the grace of God. That is not to mean that people automatically respond to the amount of knowledge and understanding that they are given concerning spiritual things, but it does mean that without the grace of God, no man can conceive of the things of God. Any revelation of Himself by God is an act of grace.

Which then brings a logical question. If God's revelation of Himself is an act of grace, why does He not reveal more than He does? Why does He leave so much to faith?

It is because, as much as God is interested in our minds, He is more interested in our wills. The person who is walking toward the end of a pier during the day when he is able to see and can determine the end, is not having to submit his will to that walk. He is walking by sight and will walk confidently to the end and stop at the edge. However, the person who is required to walk the same pier at night and who has no light by which to see where the pier ends, must force himself to take each step into the darkness. It is an act of the will; a submitting of the will to the required task. God reveals enough of Himself and creates the desire within man to cause man to come to the point where he wants to take that step into faith. Yet, God hides enough of Himself so that man's step into faith is an act of the will. A surrender to what, from the lost man's position, seems to be a step into darkness. The amazing thing about the step into darkness is that the moment it is taken, one discovers that what he thought was darkness, was in fact a step into the light.

When that step is taken, God does the marvelous act of salvation by which the man experiences the new birth. Or, more simply stated, the person is born again.

34

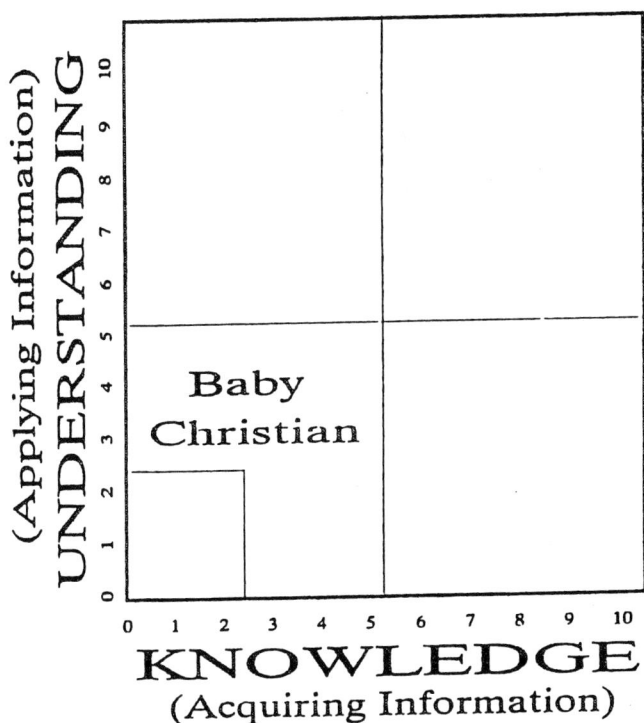

FIGURE 2

In the physical world, a birth implies a new baby. In the Christian faith, the same implication is true. The person born again is beginning his or her Christian life as a new baby in Christ. He or she has little knowledge and little understanding of what he or she knows, but the first step has been taken. That person is in the Baby Christian Quadrant (Figure 2).

God's will, however, is for Baby Christians to grow in the full knowledge and understanding of the things of God. For this to happen, new Christians must accept the responsibility to add to their own knowledge line. As they do, so they begin to move toward Quadrant Two.

CHAPTER FIVE

QUADRANT TWO:
The Pharisee Stage

Knowledge is the measurement of intelligence. One definition of intelligence is the ability to learn. However, knowledge is not the measurement of wisdom. While knowledge is a part of wisdom, it is only one part. And a part never makes a whole. One can be smart, and in that sphere of smartness, that person can know much. He or she can be a walking encyclopedia and still lack wisdom.

We all have known those who had more degrees than a thermometer who didn't have enough sense to come in from the rain. In Arkansas, we called such a person an "educated fool." Every once in a while when I do something really stupid, Wanda will remind me that I had better be careful or else folks will consider me a residence of this second quadrant.

However, though the Arkansawyers' definition has some meaning for those in this second quadrant, a better definition has already been given (Figure 3).

There were those in the Bible who possessed much knowledge and very little understanding. These men were able to quote large portions of the Old Testament by memory. In fact, they probably could quote the first five books of the Bible. Yet, in all of their knowledge, the Lord referred to them as being blind leaders of the blind. The most famous of the Pharisees to us Christians was Saul of Tarsus, better known by his Christian name, Paul. Not only is Saul the best known, he is also the best example of the personality temperaments of those in this quadrant.

The Word of God without the Spirit of God can be cold

37

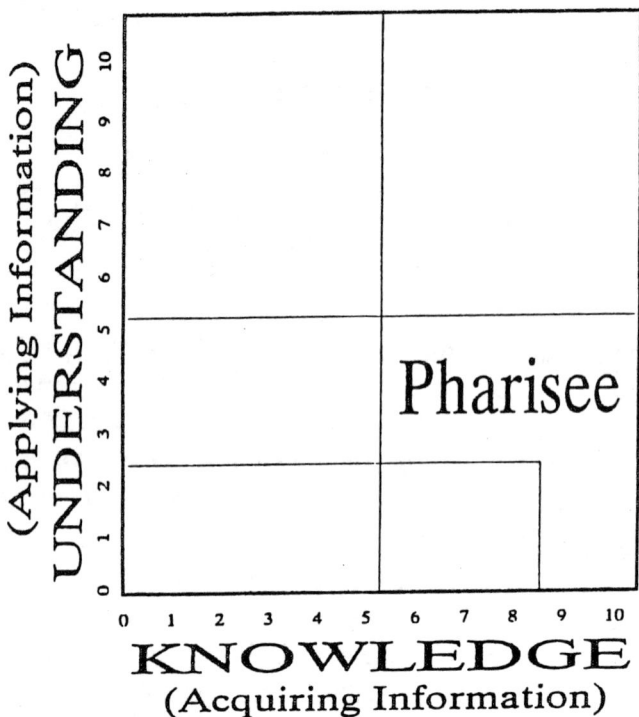

FIGURE 3

and harsh. It refers to itself as being "sharper than a two-edged sword," and it is. However, a sharp sword must be handled with care or else it can be dangerous. Note for example the temperaments of the Pharisees. They were unloving, selfish, proud, and legalistic. They had little patience for anyone who disagreed with them. They had even less for those whom they considered might have a different understanding of God from theirs, and certainly no tolerance for anyone who might be closer to God than they.

If this is so, is one to be afraid that their knowledge may exceed their understanding and therefore be dangerous? Of course not. The values of Biblical truths are seldom understood before they are known. These essentials must be learned even though their significance is not made clear at first. Till the occasion of their understanding arises later, they are to be learned and stored away.

If, however, one becomes proud of his or her knowledge, then the old proverb "A little knowledge is a dangerous thing" becomes magnified to "Much knowledge is a disastrous thing." For example, man came to a knowledge of atom power before man came to an understanding of atom power. While there is no argument in my opinion against its use in order to end World War II, the fact remains that for years two great nations stared at each other with threatening eyes with the ability to destroy civilization hidden away in silos and submarines.

I was asked to come to a church that was in the midst of a potentially splitting situation. My task was to moderate what promised to be an interesting business meeting. The sides in the disagreement were on opposite sides of the church when I called the meeting to order. Quickly one of the men stood and informed me that he had a couple of commentaries and a Bible dictionary and was the "Bible scholar of the church." Within my mind and heart, I immediately placed him in the Pharisee Quadrant, and as the meeting progressed, I realized that I was right. He had knowledge without understanding. With all his knowledge, he still lacked wisdom.

CHAPTER SIX

QUADRANT THREE:
The Sage Stage

If it is possible for one to be high in Knowledge and low in Understanding, is it possible for one to have great Understanding, but little Knowledge?

At first, it would not seem so. However, as one ponders the question, the possibility begins to surface. Not only is it a possibility, it is a fact.

An example of one's being high in Understanding while low in Knowledge is my own dad.

Dad got right with the Lord when he was thirty-six years of age. My dad was not an educated man. He could not read or write. Therefore, he was limited in the means by which he could get Knowledge of God's Word. Since he could not read, he had to depend upon other's reading the Bible to him. Mom did this each night, and immediately after our joining the church, we started having a family altar time primarily so that Mom could read the Bible aloud for my dad. There were no full time religious radio stations in our part of Arkansas, so during the working day, Dad could not listen to a gospel station. Tape players had not been developed to the extent that they are today, so Dad did not have the opportunities to listen to tapes of sermons or of the scriptures. Thus, the only time he could get into the Word was when he was in a community of either family or church. However, the lack of the ability to read did not diminish his ability to pray, and he became a tremendous man of prayer. Much time in prayer produced a high degree of spiritual maturity, even though he was limited in his knowledge of the Word of God. This spiritual maturity, or Understanding, far exceeded his Knowledge. And though I knew more scripture than did my dad, as a young preacher boy, I often went to him for advice because I valued his Understanding.

This Quadrant Three, high in Understanding, low in Knowledge Quadrant, is what I call the Sage Quadrant (Figure 4). The picture is that of the old man on the mountain whom everyone in the valley would go to when they had problems in the valley below. While it may have been years since the old sage had been in the valley, the people still valued the old sage's practical understanding of life's problems and situations. His advice was welcomed.

The source for Spiritual Knowledge is the Word of God, and it is the learner's responsibility to get as much knowledge as he or she is capable of learning. However, the source for Spiritual Understanding is the Spirit of God. The learner is not passive in the receiving of Understanding. He or she must yield to the Teacher and in submission be willing to receive Understanding through the channels by which the Spirit of God may chose to work.

Some of the channels by which Understanding can come are similar to those through which Knowledge can come. For example, there is more preaching done today, I believe, on godly principles than there were when I was a boy. God's principles are an expression of Biblical truths. They are expressions of application of spiritual information, and as such fall more into the Understanding mode than they do in the Knowledge mode. One can know a Biblical principle, but it is only when it is applied that the principle actually is activated in the person's life. This application is the beginning of Understanding. Therefore, I can be taught by the Spirit of God working in the teaching and preaching ministries of

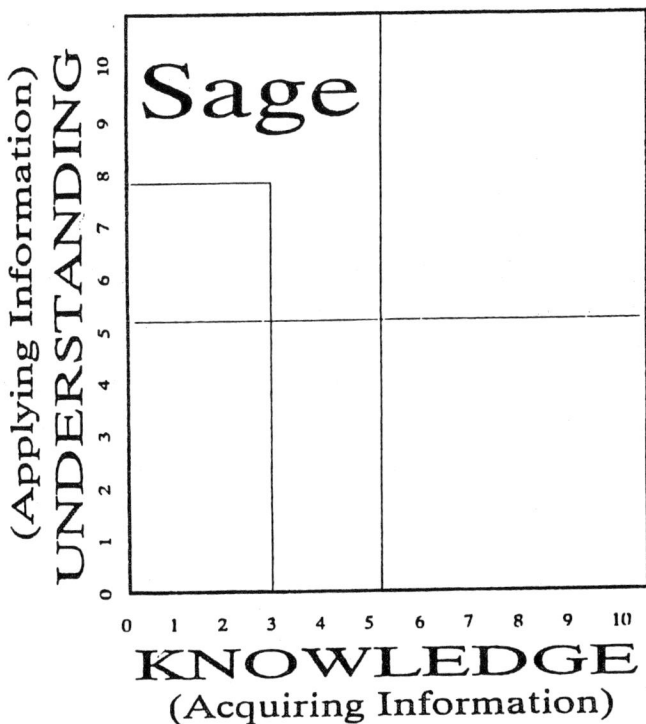

Y-axis: (Applying Information) UNDERSTANDING — 0 1 2 3 4 5 6 7 8 9 10

X-axis: 0 1 2 3 4 5 6 7 8 9 10

Sage

KNOWLEDGE
(Acquiring Information)

FIGURE 4

others.

The Spirit of God can teach me through circumstances, through my inner conscience, and can be my teacher as I study the Word of God. A passage which I have known for a long time, may suddenly become clear in a way that I had never known before, because of my Holy teacher.

One thing that develops between a teacher and a student is the student's tendency to take on the characteristics of his or her teacher. Especially is this true if the student has a great deal of love and respect for the teacher.

The fruit, or characteristics, of the Spirit of God as listed in Galatians 5:22-23 are love, joy, peace, longsuffering, gentleness, goodness, faith, meekness, and temperance. As one is under the influence of the Holy Teacher, one will began to develop the fruit of the Spirit into his or her life.

Amazingly, one of the major secular studies done on wisdom has acknowledged that wisdom does contain a personality element. In the effort to identify what that personality element is, the study did extensive research in an effort to identify it. All they needed to do was to study the eternal truths of God's word, and they would have found it in Galatians chapter five.

There was a time when the rural church could be associated with an uneducated membership, but that is no longer the case. However, in those early days of my ministry when so much of my work was done in small rural churches, I found some fantastic men and women. These saints would have been considered limited in their knowledge, but they had an understanding of God's Word and work that blessed my life over and over again. They were true residents of the Sage Quadrant.

CHAPTER SEVEN

QUADRANT FOUR:
The Wisdom Stage

In the cartoon B.C., cartoonist Hart has Wiley's Dictionary give a definition for "Wisdom." He wrote, "Wisdom is what--if you need to know the definition of--you ain't got."

If this is true, then most educators are not wise. During the past few years, there has been a renewed interest in the subject of "Wisdom." The direction of most of the studies has been to define "Wisdom." Several suggestions have been made, but none that has been wholeheartedly accepted by the academic community.

All the researchers I have found seem to be in agreement that Wisdom is composed of at least two different components. And though all agree that Knowledge is one of the components, there is wide disagreement as to what the other component or components are.

It is amazing how close the secular writers have come to the Essential Truth that Wisdom's second component is Understanding. One interesting study suggested that the individual's personality is involved in the achievement of Wisdom. This study suggested that few hateful, mean, antisocial, unkind, or spiteful person are considered "wise." These persons may be considered "smart," or "intelligent," but not "wise." While the study had no answer for the development of these good people-skill temperaments, their findings did confirm an Understanding characteristic.

Note the characteristics of godly Wisdom as recorded by James in chapter three, *But the wisdom that is from above is first pure, then peaceable, gentle, and easy to be intreated, full of mercy, and good fruits, without partiality, and without hypocrisy.* How similar these are to the fruit of the spirit as recorded in Galatians 5, . . . *fruit of the Spirit is love, joy, peace, longsuffering, gentleness, goodness, faith, meekness, temperance.*

The person who grows in Understanding being taught by the Spirit of God and developing the Knowledge gained from the Word of God will development the character of God.

Wisdom, then, is a special gift given by God to those who are especially prepared. If I would be wise, I must prepare myself by adding to my reservoir of Knowledge. I must never feel that I "have arrived," but instead I must realize that learning is to be a life-long endeavor. But, not only must I add to my reservoir of Knowledge, I must yield myself to the Holy Spirit of God and be open to His leadership and teachership. If I would know of God, I must study His Word; if I would know God, I must yield to His Spirit.

And one of the amazing paradoxes of the Christian faith is that the more we yield, the more we gain. The more dependent we become on God, the more independent we become to the world. The more God-sufficient we become, the more self-sufficient we seem to be to others. The more we confess ourselves as children to God, the more the world sees us as mature. The more we see ourselves as foolish in relationship to His Wisdom, the more others will see us as Wise in relationship to the wisdom of the world (Figure 5).

Godly Wisdom produces leadership in those to whom it is given. *Who is a wise man and endued with knowledge among you? Let him shew out of a good conversation his works with meekness of wisdom,* James 3:13. The wise person does not announce his or her wisdom, but instead it is seen by their style of life and their works done in a naturally humble manner.

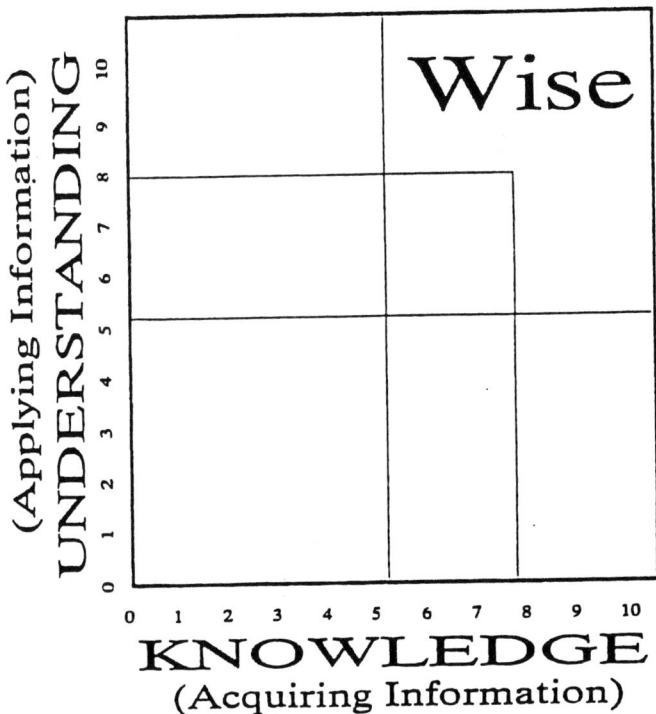

FIGURE 5

Last of all, the wise person will be a teacher. The classroom may or may not be the formal classroom, but the wise person will be a teacher nonetheless. As James states in the verse quoted previously, the wise person's lifestyle will of itself be a teaching tool.

If any man lacks wisdom . . . James wrote. Most of us would have to confess that wisdom is not one of our characteristics. Yet, God implies that it should be. What a challenge to Christian growth.

Some day people will speak of me in the past tense. They will be saying, "Ernie was . . ." It is my prayer that when they are speaking of me in the past tense form of the verb, that someone, somewhere, may say, "You know . . . he was a wise man."